CREATING A BUDGET
Made Simple

FAMILY BUDGETING MADE FUN

Financial Empowerment is a Family Affair

Dr. Rosie Milligan

Professional Publishing House
1425 W. Manchester Ave., Ste. B
Los Angeles, California 90047
323-750-3592
Email: professionalpublishinghouse@yahoo.com
www.Professionalpublishinghouse.com

Cover design: TWASolutions.com
First printing December 2016
978-0-9983089-1-3
10987654321

For inquiries contact: drrosie@aol.com

Financial Empowerment is a Family Affair

Families are at each other's throats, marriages are on the rocks, and many illnesses are caused by the stress and burden of the lack of money and being head-over-heels in debt. A well-structured budget includes input from each family member. A budget provides insight into what you are currently spending and what you can cut from the budget and still be okay. A budget is the blueprint/road map that leads you to financial freedom.

Books On Business & Finance
by Dr. Rosie Milligan

1. Getting Out Of Debt Made Simple

2. Understanding Credit Made Simple

3. Creating A Budget Made Simple

4. What You Need To Know Before You Start A Business

5. Departing This Life Preparations: Everything You Need To Know To Get Your Personal And   Business Affairs In Order

For other books by Dr. Rosie Milligan,
visit Drrosie.com.

FAMILY BUDGETING
MADE FUN

Let's start taking inventory. Remember, there are no more secrets. If a past due notice comes in the mail, it's everybody's business. Don't carry the burden of financial pressure alone. It is much easier when you share it. You will be surprised to know that family members have the solution to many of your problems that cause so much stress and pain, if you would only let them help you carry your burden.

You are probably thinking you don't want your problems to become your family's problem. Your family can appreciate you more when they know why your behavior is abnormal. Whether you want to admit it or not—when burdened with bills, your outgoing is more than your incoming, creditors are calling at home and work—your behavior becomes a little strange.

Start taking inventory by going through your checkbook to see where your money is going. Make a list, and call it "Where Did My Money Go?" Make two columns. In the right column, list all bills, house expenses, personal, and miscellaneous, etc. In the left column, list all the interest paid for the month. To find the interest, look on your mortgage statement and your monthly bills statements. It is so important to look at the amount of interest paid every month. If you look at it every month, you will quickly decide to take some constructive actions. Make a list of all income for the household with three columns: Depending Monies, Sometimes Monies, and Miscellaneous Monies. Include money from each family member. Look at what you *must* give up, not what you *want* to give up.

A BUDGET IS IMPORTANT NO MATTER HOW SMALL YOUR INCOME MAY BE

It is good practice to do an annual (yearly) budget in December for the upcoming year. You should do a monthly budget first. Every month will be different, because some expenses occur on a seasonal basis. For example: birthdays, special occasions, graduations, proms, Christmas, weddings, vacations, tuitions, etc.

A planned monthly budget gives you foresight instead of hindsight. The monthly budget in this book covers most expenses that will occur in any given month. Each month's budget should take into consideration family goals and dream lists. The next few pages will give a guideline for a Family Monthly Budget.

MONTHLY BUDGET

Net Wages After Taxes $ _____

Other Income   _____

_____   _____

_____   _____

_____   _____

_____   _____

_____   _____

TOTAL INCOME $ _____

EXPENSES:

Rent/Mortgage   _____

Electric   _____

Water Co.   _____

Gas Co.   _____

Telephone   _____

    Cell Phone   _____

    Over-the limit charges on
      cell phone   _____

    Information charges from
      telephone operator   _____

Groceries

    Food items   _____

    Non-food items   _____

Insurance

    Life   _____

    Health (medical)   _____

    Disability   _____

    Long-Term   _____

    Auto   _____

    Home   _____

Automobile

 Payment or lease _____

 Gas, oil, etc. _____

 Maintenance _____

 Insurance _____

Childcare _____

Installment Payment

 Credit Cards _____

 Installment Loans _____

 Educational Loans _____

Clothing

 Purchase _____

 Laundry _____

 Pampers or Diapers _____

 Dry Cleaning _____

Recreation & Entertainment

Events   _____

Dining out   _____

Lunch at work   _____

Vacations   _____

Video rentals   _____

Gyms & spas   _____

Education

Tuition   _____

Books & Tapes   _____

Seminars   _____

Organizational

Dues   _____

Subscriptions   _____

Church

Tithes   _____

Offering   _____

Church (cont'd)

    Special Events   _____

    Uniforms, etc.   _____

Personal Care

    Routine Dr. visits   _____

    Physical   _____

    Dentist   _____

    Hair Care   _____

    Nails   _____

    Cosmetics   _____

Bottle Water   _____

Gardener   _____

Bus pass   _____

Children's school allowance   _____

Special Occasions

Christmas gifts   _____

Birthdays   _____

Mother's Day   _____

Father's Day   _____

Bridal Showers/
  Wedding Gifts   _____

Graduations   _____

Proms   _____

Class ring   _____

School jacket   _____

Miscellaneous

Banquet tickets   _____

Raffle tickets   _____

BBQ Dinners   _____

Candy drives   _____

Patron list   _____

TOTAL EXPENSES $ _____

AVERAGE/SHORTAGE $ _____

Once the family budget is completed, it is not enough to say, "Here it is." Each family member must be willing to make changes. To achieve financial freedom, each family member must make a commitment to the project.

If you want conditions to change in your life, you must change. Remember, if you keep on doing what you have been doing, you will keep on getting what you have been getting. The following page is a commitment for you and your family members to complete. When each member has to complete this worksheet, schedule a time to discuss each commitment.

MY COMMITMENT

"I know if I keep on doing what I have been doing, I will keep on getting what I've been getting."

Things I will do to help cut down on expenses and to help save money.

_____

_____

_____

_____

_____

My contributions to the project:

1.

2.

3.

4.

CONGRATULATIONS!

You have completed a great accomplishment. Now, you have the most important job left to do—see if what you've been doing is working for you. It's evaluation time!

You and each family member must complete a monthly evaluation form. You should schedule a time for family discussion.

The evaluation gives you a chance to modify plans and goals, if necessary. You might need to make your twelve-month goals, two-year goals, etc.

The following page is a Monthly Progress Evaluation Form.

MONTHLY PROGRESS EVALUATION FORM

- I did all things I said I would do to help.

- I did some of the things I said I would do to help.

- I did more than what I said I would do to help.

- I see where I can do much more to help.

List the results you can see, at this point, from your team effort.

_____

_____

_____

_____

_____

_____

_____

_____

_____

_____

_____

List additional things you will do next month to help.

_____

_____

_____

_____

_____

_____

_____

_____

_____

_____

How much money did the family some from my efforts?

_____

_____

_____

_____

_____

_____

_____

21 WAYS TO SAVE MONEY WITHOUT INCREASING YOUR INCOME

1. Purchase a cell phone where there is no charge to you for incoming calls.

2. Do not allow your gasoline tank drop below a quarter of a tank; your car uses more gas when this occurs, and this can also lead to a burned-out fuel pump.

3. Use Google search for telephone numbers versus dialing 411, which costs.

4. Plan a weekly menu. Make a grocery list before grocery shopping. When shopping, stick to your list.

5. Learn ways to create a new dish from leftovers and make it taste fresh & new.

6. Use shopping coupons when grocery shopping.

7. Do bulk shopping with a family member/friend when purchasing items such as toilet tissue, paper towels, Kleenex, etc.

8. Wash a full load of clothes when washing versus everybody in the house washing a few pieces at a time.

9. Save on gasoline by mapping out your travel route before you get started each day with errands/chores.

10. Purchase automobile insurance with a $500–$1,000 deductible. As you know, in most cases, people do not report damage under $500 for fear of an insurance rate increase—so why pay extra?

11. Pay off credit cards with the highest interest rates first or switch outstanding credit cards with a high interest rate to a card with a low interest rate. Place the interest saved in a savings account.

12. Purchase items like an electric heater or fan during off-season when they are less expensive.

13. Recycle bottles, cans, etc. A little can add up to a lot, and you will be quite surprised about how much money your recycling can turn into.

14. Invest in a water system rather than buying single bottles of water. It will pay off in the long run.

15. Do not discard purses and shoes that can be repaired. Take them to a shoe repair shop.

16. Eat leftovers for lunch.

17. Repair leaky faucets and any other water drippings.

18. Purchase an outside sensor light instead of leaving the porch light burning all night.

19. Weather-strip your windows and doors.

20. Find an honest mechanic and have your car serviced. The minute you hear unusual noises or sounds, have your car checked out. Learn how to check your engine oil and change it periodically. *It's cheaper to fix a little problem before it turns into a big problem. Your car is the next largest*

investment after your home, and you will need a car most of your life, so treat it like an investment—watch over it and manage it well.

21.   **Tips for saving at the gas pump**. (1) Slow your roll, speed eats up your fuel. Driving 5 miles over 60 mph, is like paying .30 extra for every gallon of gas you burn. (2)Do not load you car down with items such as: flags, bikes, carriers, luggage, racks, etc. Excess weight makes the engine work harder, increases drag which causes wasting of fuel. Close your car window when driving at high speed, this causes drag and wasting of fuel too. (3)Be a smooth operator. Avoid jerking, frequent accelerating when trying to go around and pass other vehicles and frequent jamming on your brakes. This alone can save you $1.00 or more per gallon of gasoline---this can make a financial difference. (4)Avoid idling of your car; 15 minutes of idling can burn a quarter of a gallon of gasoline.

Don't be afraid to get your hands a little dirty. Learn to check and to change your wiper blades, check belts and hoses for wear, clean the dirt and dust from the engine's air-filter, the dirt and dust clogs up the filter and causes the car to use more gasoline.

Order Form

BOOKS ON FINANCE BY DR. ROSIE MILLIGAN

TITLE	PRICE		QTY		TOTAL
Getting Out of Debt Made Simple	$10.00	x	___	=	_____
Understanding Credit Made Simple	$10.00	x	___	=	_____
Creating A Budget Made Simple	$5.00	x	___	=	_____
What You Need To Know Before You Start A Business	$15.00	x	___	=	_____
Departing This Life Preparations: Everything	$12.00	x	___	=	_____

You Need To Know To Get Your Personal & Business Affairs In Order

Shipping: **$6.45**
(add $1.00 each add'l book)

TOTAL DUE _____

Payment/Customer Information

$_____ Due in check or money order

Name: _____
Address: _____
City: _____ State: _____ ZIP: _____
Phone: _____
E-mail: _____

Send Order Form and Payment to:

Professional Publishing House
1425 W. Manchester Ave., Ste. B
Los Angeles, California 90047